SIDEBROW BOOKS

THE WINE-DARK SEA

Published by Sidebrow Books
P.O. Box 86921
Portland, OR 97286
sidebrow@sidebrow.net
www.sidebrow.net

Cover art by Josh Keyes
Cover design by Jason & Felix Snyder
Book design by Jason Snyder

ISBN: 1-940090-05-9
ISBN-13: 978-1-940090-05-4

FIRST EDITION | FIRST PRINTING
9 8 7 6 5 4 3 2 1
SIDEBROW BOOKS 016
PRINTED IN THE UNITED STATES

Sidebrow Books titles are distributed by
Small Press Distribution

Titles are available directly from Sidebrow at
www.sidebrow.net/books

A Member of
inter
section
incubator
Services for Artists
www.theintersection.org

Sidebrow is a member of the Intersection Incubator, a program of
Intersection for the Arts (www.theintersection.org) providing fiscal
sponsorship, incubation, and consulting for artists. Contributions
to Sidebrow are tax-deductible to the extent allowed by law.

THE WINE-DARK SEA

MATHIAS SVALINA

SIDEBROW BOOKS + 2016 + PORTLAND & SAN FRANCISCO

for Selah Saterstrom

It is a convenience not to fear the dark.

—Diogenes
(tr. Guy Davenport)

THE WINE-DARK SEA

Knowing suffering
is a liturgy.

Knowing the eyeless
we grow more eyes.

Just think: your
own hand
is always awake.

I want to show you
what I saw
in the glass.

Let's unbury everything
clotted
with nests.

THE WINE-DARK SEA

I am trying
to be simple as ink.

I talk to you
sometimes
in the daylight.

At night
I try not to
suspend.

There is so much
I can't form
that is true.

Celan said this
to Ilana Shmueli:

Through you I translate you over to me.

THE WINE-DARK SEA

I want
what the date wants
from its box,
printed in lip.

The concerto
cast a morning
beneath bridges
where ropes dangle.

I cannot stand
inside myself.

What emerged
when I opened my mouth
was a thanking tomb.

So we tremble.
Do we tremble?

We tremble.

THE WINE-DARK SEA

Asking is easy
for a number.

Words are burdens.
Mouths lumber.

I should not be afraid
of myself:

a little perpetuity
with arms,

a comb with teeth
bent back.

Around me the white
draws a ring,
a one.

THE WINE-DARK SEA

The hum, yes,
that corruption.

That rot
at play.

Beneath me,
Easter.

Meanwhile,
a PO box.

THE WINE-DARK SEA

I almost died

like a letter
never posted.

Glue brittle.

I needed it later
but by then

each word
quivered
in quotation marks.

THE WINE-DARK SEA

I breathe
with gate &

I breathe
with light

& not only with it.

This is repetition.

I breathe the
uninterruptible law

of no money
that we really love.

THE WINE-DARK SEA

So close
to the river

trucks & insects
combine.

In the river
I'd be a difference,

orange plastic bag,
a catalog.

each morning
moonceasing.

THE WINE-DARK SEA

Lain down wirebent,
night margins
a bed full
of rain
in scriptorium walls.

I'd like
to title
this next chapter
"The Quiet Storm."

I am making an effort
at humanity.

THE WINE-DARK SEA

First there is not enough water
& then too much.

The day eternal
& then asphalt spills
into the caesura.

The whole mess
fidgets there.

I live toward that.

THE WINE-DARK SEA

My utopia opens
from both directions:
the beautiful line,
the glossy rind.

My problem is
I've never not been able
to write.

THE WINE-DARK SEA

Enter any blackness
& emerge in any nowhere.

The location changes but
there is only blood's nowhere.

THE WINE-DARK SEA

Memory draws back
dialing lips.
These unreal

reasons to write,
to say, straight true.

It is already a month
since I left
the hospital.

Like everything in letters
there is a little
& a ligature.

THE WINE-DARK SEA

The with
memory upends,
the unchangingness.

Return to ants
swarming legs,
urine on the kitchen floor,

to bent pine,
a trachea-nowhere:

the thing I
body contains

spokes
in such varied
panic.

THE WINE-DARK SEA

I dig three points
in the frozen dirt & set
a small fire inside.

Wherever there are two things
there are three things.

THE WINE-DARK SEA

I am on the island
that speaks a language
I can only understand,

where a wish
is anything rotting,
the shore.

THE WINE-DARK SEA

Let us not count days.
I drink from both sides of the glass.

There is a sickness
& below, only
violin strings, accord,

& below, the dust & degree.
It is more horrible to imagine
than to see it.

We do this
every day.

THE WINE-DARK SEA

Yes. Appear
nightsun.

Downtown lights
loom & patients
down their pills.

I am turning
but where is it going?

I need a chord
of bright light.
Not a disappearance.

It is waiting.

THE WINE-DARK SEA

I wanted nothing.
And never got it.

And now I want to want
a home for homes.

What was missing
was an of-margin,

a long work
of logic.

Desire is precarious.
Eventually I did that.

THE WINE-DARK SEA

Brightly lit,
an ageless crawling sun:
error is not the problem.

Another debt,
another bomb scare,

a window propped
with a soup can.

Surveillance,
punishment,
shame:

why are you so small
Marx, Freud, Rimbaud, etc. ?

THE WINE-DARK SEA

The wrinkles around my eyes
& my cracked teeth:

finally
some objective facts.

What I am scared of most
is never transmitted.

If I had will
I'd be dead.

I can't remember when
I decided I would kill myself.

It happened all at once,
not like a levee breaking,

like a car,

at the end of a workday,
turning off the road
& into a driveway.

THE WINE-DARK SEA

This emptiness pulses
like a stick.

I try to think with,

feel clouds in each
paper. Again,

these long days of white moths
rising. I don't want
to give up.

I am thinking,
dayskin,
always thinking.

THE WINE-DARK SEA

Bones speak
the narrowness of dark.

It's hard to be seen
through microscopes.
It is hard.

It is
the doubled exile of home.

My hands,
my face,
those too an opening.

Hold me in you.

THE WINE-DARK SEA

Nothing moves
to cross the day.

Please, one thing,
simply reap a meaning.

Call it stammering,
call it *self*,

the writing descending
into its own sea.

To say its name
takes so much mouth

& all I say
satiates.

Toward is true.
Neverleave is true.

As are the willow threads
the suns shed.

THE WINE-DARK SEA

All of you
offers up all of you.

Once I was pieces
& now I am a question
with two pulses.

You have such dark blood.
Dark & hot
twine into & out of you.

The line of your throat
disembranches from your chest:

Sonnet 115.

THE WINE-DARK SEA

Before my name
there were other names
& after mine
the same.

Is this blockage
of all thoughts and
memories something passing?

We ride thinking
in the heart,
calm, all riding all
others.

Make of margins.

THE WINE-DARK SEA

Memory
spun me
wintersound.

These are notes,
a box of nails
& land-locked

to work your
motor face
to face.

THE WINE-DARK SEA

What's one region
in an age

of containment?
Before the cenotaph?

Every question
a bone function.

Every suffering
a center.

Every morning
I try to be

there,
now,

un-corner.

THE WINE-DARK SEA

Each day emerges
in apprise.

No one
can be
companion—

the grass

purely
containment.

I enter so clearly
an undetectable
plea.

And then—
is this self-evident?—
the blade itself
stains the paper.

THE WINE-DARK SEA

Make a noise
& there is no
predicting

what some char
to war poem
or worship.

Is this a landscape yet
or only lyric's
linger?
Surprise chains

like drying
skin.

Make a noise.
Don't worry.
It stays forever.

THE WINE-DARK SEA

This tone-deafness,
this joy of tone-deafness,
cisterns me.

The shape of
language is vigilance.

You.
You are your face.
Your face.

Brain on cement.

The exit from
ink & control.
I know.

THE WINE-DARK SEA

It's harder to tell
where the world ends.
I can't think without Julia
so Julia is my mind.

Julia is my mind.
Robert is my mind.
Zach is my mind.
Jon is my mind.
Heather is my mind.
Josh is my mind.
Sara is my mind.
Dave is my mind.
Teal is my mind.
Sommer is my mind.
Noah is my mind.

In the sun I carry
everyone I know & I
am carried on their backs.

They are the wine-dark sea. And I
am the wine-dark sea.

THE WINE-DARK SEA

The lamplight
returns me:

knotted memory,
the view

from the top
of the sunrise

parking-garage,
the city clean

by morning
like a cone.

No ideas,
in this night

perpetual, only
answerings.

THE WINE-DARK SEA

I need to need
how a tree
holds the dirt.

When you hold
me, a government.

The doomed duty.
The ditto.

I'm astonished you
still hold me, Zach.

Me & these bees,
& stagnancy.

THE WINE-DARK SEA

Stone circles light,
trembling an end.

Who made my mouth
of this lead?

I made my mouth
of this lead,

this trembling medicine,
an alley unsaid.

THE WINE-DARK SEA

My death, dear
as a ring

I can't stop turning
round my finger.

I hold it up to strangers
saying: *She loves me.*

Does she love me?
Does she love the asphalt?

THE WINE-DARK SEA

A skull
makes a puzzle
of meaning.

My mind
is a double-song
of caves—

memory
is dangerous.

I wanted
a maw
& got a scattering.

Ash, an agent.
Fill it with light.

Open the wound
of the sea
for which there are no songs.

THE WINE-DARK SEA

Nightnoise, immense,
of secret thinking,
collides with
what dark tolls.

Serial choirs,
pretty monsters,
waiting
to break the silence
like a strangling.

All this pain
in orbit, making
us the center,
an unlipped song.

THE WINE-DARK SEA

A garden rises

from the mirror,
the sea.

Why shouldn't death
feel assuring?

A field of sighs,
chatter wilted,
borne.

THE WINE-DARK SEA

In a dream I tell Sommer
I must return to the hospital.

I say *I must return to the hospital*
like an ant eating its own body.

Sommer says *We can never*
understand the actual joy of the world.

I hide inside
a game closet.

It is morning
on July 9, 2011.

For three months I have
been trying not to die.

THE WINE-DARK SEA

I try to write myself
a price tag:
shadowfete.

I always assumed
I'd die alone
on the edge
of a page,

flesh so soft
a fingernail would
burst the skin.

THE WINE-DARK SEA

Keep the camera close
to search folds of fact.

Keep the neat trick
of sunlight

on the backseat
of the object.

But what makes me weep
about the movie

is seeing Noah weep,
& the unbehavable way

art makes buying onions
so demanding.

THE WINE-DARK SEA

Of my hand,
of dew-urges,
of sand found

in an old suitcase,
I have only
recitations.

The mind edits memory
into uniforms even
the moon can see.

THE WINE-DARK SEA

The ideas
only words direct.

Out dying between
the moment &
saying it:

a den against day,
a palpitate night the
mouth makes outside.

THE WINE-DARK SEA

Too long
stormwater
anything.

Pills go down
& return

in verse.
Nothing fits

without another thing
emptying.

I tear skin from my
fingers with my teeth.

THE WINE-DARK SEA

My first teacher
was a burning.

I change skins.
It is a nursery.

I see my father
incoherent

in the moment
of his death.

I see the settling
of the blood
beneath the skin.

I see the sun
in his chest.

My mother in white.
I vanish as I appear.

I open my mouth
& stone spills out.

THE WINE-DARK SEA

I break
& break myself

again. Until

the crack of bone
is the name
I degree.

Imagine something
perfectly round.

Then cut it
in half & imagine

it again.

THE WINE-DARK SEA

I can't need
beyond germ

& what can
poetry save?

Another mountain
stripped to a bowl.

Inside this
rot & yet I

survive,
nightnothing.

When I was not here
you were here.

Speaksalt
night.

THE WINE-DARK SEA

The night

only sees
ocean.

Find yourself
inside yourself,
my self,

a stone,

a cut across
my thumbprint

stains the
whole night

frost.

THE WINE-DARK SEA

The tremblings
again merge

& cut

meat
numb.

Verb the ditch
of arcing,
of hiding,

monotony
of morning.

THE WINE-DARK SEA

Lurch & rush,
agape this,
agape that.

A kaleidoscope
in nightcoughs

held up
by lips.

Writing solves a nothing.
Vocation. A stone eye

sees itself in
any stone.

THE WINE-DARK SEA

A grave
language is
permitted to forget.

There is no betrayal
in accuracy.

Soft for
pills —
I can't let emptiness
inside.

Beaten to
jet,

what I break into two
is not broken.

THE WINE-DARK SEA

I stack sea like bags of stone
into the hole into which
I am always falling.

In webbed light,
whither trembling?
whither bone's astonishment?

Veins vein
the shore.

Tumor mouth.
Hole ink.

Any key fits any lock.

THE WINE-DARK SEA

Whatever marks me
is me.

I hide
beneath the spine
of sentence.

We make the world ourselves:
night signs the ice
that floats.

When driving
I see a baby horse

in a fenced-in field,
standing in its own shadow.

THE WINE-DARK SEA

Sun pinks
the foothills, I wait
for the street below to clear
& listen to *A Love Supreme*.

Morning breeze shakes
the fringe of my scarf,
my father's scarf.

When I close my eyes
I am anywhere,
all doors slamming.

THE WINE-DARK SEA

This token of light.
This map-noise.

Too much me,
suckling night's
emptyings.

Shelley in my
left hand

pills
in the right.

What happens inside
love that's so hollowing?

THE WINE-DARK SEA

The twisting
of resistance
wears me out.

Yet water
continues to reflect
the black pain
of mountains.

In deathgains,
o animal.

There is only so far
one can stretch a scar.

THE WINE-DARK SEA

Every hope fallows
differently.

What was once a city
is now a series
of stories:

the garden,

the dying garden,

nothing is so
slow as beauty.

THE WINE-DARK SEA

Wade waist-deep
into the freezing water

in the cave.

Hold still for
the flash.

I know every letter
in this book
by the throat.

When the drugs wear off
I am the car
beneath the tarp.

THE WINE-DARK SEA

Exit this poem for me.

Show me a way.

THE WINE-DARK SEA

This bowl of blood
only works
for the dead.

We fold the world
in half
like a napkin.

It's a lurching world of etceteras
but all these books can't
stop a stripmine.

No rudder,
no ship.

THE WINE-DARK SEA

Who is this

wandering
among seeds?

Every virtue unsays itself.

I love you,
I love you,
what is this

rutting through caves
of cut glass?

THE WINE-DARK SEA

When I don't know
what I know

even my flesh
is white.

THE WINE-DARK SEA

Skip still,
swimming
awful eyes.

A wish of
bravery &
bravery.

Stop looking.

Dine on dust
& lice & ash,

comma,
comma, period.

THE WINE-DARK SEA

Ropewant,
eking,
until no cars come.

Two is all
I can make
of memory,

cloud-dizzy.

Ornate mold
of word.

The only warden
can I afford.

THE WINE-DARK SEA

Of the noises I've been
I find the table
most inaudible

muttering *knife,*
knife, knife.

Say not
the lamp goes out

but
the lamp goes out by itself.

THE WINE-DARK SEA

Silence stitches
sickness.

Broken back-together meat
like dead fish in
a fishbowl,

glass shattering
each morning.

I'm at the treeline.
I'm rising above it.

THE WINE-DARK SEA

This road walks
heart-unformed.

Knotted signature
of water. Suspended

like a stockpile
I want to not live in.

THE WINE-DARK SEA

My need to not
be near anything—

how a choked
throat sings
only numbers.

I repeat
my choke on
alleys & stems.

An urn
in a brick wall.

THE WINE-DARK SEA

I feel spines
crack in my hands,
though I am now awake,
drinking tea from a mug
the size of my fist.

Kind pursuit.
Kind masters.
What is
gains night.

Every wrong
is always wrong.

THE WINE-DARK SEA

In unmost solaces,

I stunt each
word, paused
to the bridge.

Scars, trinkets,
images, whatever.

I can't even watch stones fall now.

THE WINE-DARK SEA

I don't understand
why blood dries.

Abracadabra:
woodsong.

I am the cage,
a song

of bruise-ash.

One must earn
the I its cage.

Desire,
degree, the I.

THE WINE-DARK SEA

In these holy days
of ditch & feast,

of the festival
of spines,

I bless
the festival.

THE WINE-DARK SEA

I reach for the kerosene of stars.
For a frail dictionary.

I wear three
layers of maps.

Each must reach
each night
until an I is a mark.

Anything: umber, sickness,
self or harm.

This is a geyser religion.
I'm the bagman.

THE WINE-DARK SEA

I knew you
in the sky.

A name hour.
A name sky.

Two piles of crumbs
before two open doors.

The sea, changeless, rises
daily from the dead

in the trembling
of the dumbtrack again-today.

THE WINE-DARK SEA

Wet bodies
burst
in the sun.

I need new songs
to bite this lip off

to find the more
fragile lip.

I can only
canopy,

the song always on

the radio,
the radio

always on.

Mathias Svalina is the author of four previous books, including *Wastoid*, *I Am A Very Productive Entrepreneur*, & *Destruction Myth*. He lives in Denver, Colorado, where he is an editor for Octopus Books & runs a Dream Delivery Service.

Parts of *The Wine-Dark Sea* were published in *Blackbird*, *Diode*, *Gulf Coast*, *Versal*, *The Volta*, & *The Volta Book of Poets* (Sidebrow Books).